D0516170

THE Mummy

monster Chronicles

STEPHEN KRENSKY

 Lerner Publications Company · M

Lerner Publications Company
A division of Lerner Publishing Group
241 First Avenue North
Minneapolis, MN 55401 U.S.A.

Website address: www.lernerbooks.com

Library of Congress Cataloging-in-Publication Data

Krensky, Stephen.
      The mummy / by Stephen Krensky.
         p.   cm. — (Monster chronicles)
      Includes bibliographical references and index.
      ISBN-13: 978-0-8225-5924-5 (lib. bdg. : alk. paper)
      ISBN-10: 0-8225-5924-2 (lib. bdg. : alk. paper)
         1. Mummies—Egypt—Juvenile literature. 2. Mummies—Juvenile literature.
      3. Mummy films—History and criticism—Juvenile literature. 4. Mummies in
      literature—Juvenile literature. I. Title. II. Series.
      DT62.M7.K74 2007
      393'.309—dc22   2005034993

Manufactured in the United States of America
1 2 3 4 5 6 - JR - 12 11 10 09 08 07

TABLE OF CONTENTS

1. Death Is Just the Beginning

6

2. Egypt Leads the Way

14

3. Mummies on the Move

24

4. Are You My Mummy?

32

Source Note

44

Selected Bibliography

44

Further Reading and Websites

44

Movies

46

Index

47

Death Is Just the Beginning

What's the scariest thing you can think of? Snakes? Spiders? Heights or small spaces? If you have an active imagination, maybe it's ghosts. Even worse, it may be the nightmarish creature that lives under your bed.

For a lot of people, though, the scariest thing is death. This fear makes sense. Death seems so final, so definite. There's no turning back. Everything is gone—especially you.

But where have you gone exactly? What happens to people once they stop living? People have always struggled to answer these questions.

Over time, people in different cultures have developed complex ideas about death. Many people believe in an afterlife—or life after death. They believe that souls move on to another place after life ends. What if they are right? What if planning for death is more like planning to move? You pack your favorite clothing and furniture and even your pets. Death is not an ending. It is simply a very big change of address.

MUMMIES MAKE AN APPEARANCE

In many ancient cultures, people took great care in preparing the dead for the afterlife. In some cultures, people mummified the dead—that is, they turned them into mummies. If you've ever seen a mummy movie, you might think a mummy is a bandaged figure marching stiffly with arms outstretched. You might think mummies are unhappy dead people who come back to life for revenge or power.

In reality, mummies are simply dead bodies. But mummies are still special. Dead people who are not mummies decay, or rot, over time. Everything in their bodies eventually turns to dust. This decay doesn't happen to mummies.

To become a mummy, a dead body must be preserved, or treated, so that it doesn't decay. Preserving dead bodies has been going on for a long time. How do we know? Because some mummies are at least ten thousand years old. They are far older than written languages and recorded history.

And mummies have been found in many different places. There are South American mummies from Peru, Chile, and Colombia. Some mummies come from China and Egypt. Others come from Siberia in Russia. There are also mummies from Denmark and Great Britain. Other mummies come from southern Europe and Egypt.

FROZEN IN TIME

In 1991 hikers found an extremely well-preserved mummy (above) in the Italian Alps. The man had died and was frozen there more than five thousand years ago. He was so well preserved that scientists were able to learn much about his life and surroundings. Scientists even found the remains of meat and bread inside his stomach.

But not all mummies are the same. Some mummies are made on purpose, and others are made by accident. Some mummies come from hot, dry places. Others come from cold, wet places. People have found some mummies inside caves or buried under the desert sand. People have found other mummies frozen in the ice. They have also found mummies buried in bogs (wet areas filled with spongy soil).

Bodies left in a bog might turn into mummies (*below*). But not every bog is right for making mummies. The bog must contain the right amount of water and a chemical called tannic acid. And the water must be close to freezing—cold enough to prevent decay.

There are even modern-day mummies. Some famous twentieth-century leaders were made into mummies after death. Mao Zedong, a Chinese ruler, and Vladimir Lenin, founder of the Soviet Union, were both mummified. However, the men were not wrapped in bandages like some other kinds of mummies. Their preserved bodies were left uncovered, so their followers could look at them for inspiration, even after death.

The mummified body of Vladimir Lenin lies in a tomb in Red Square in Moscow.

TRIP TO THE AFTERLIFE

To live well in the afterlife, a mummy needed the right supplies. So warrior tribes from northern Europe buried their mummies with weapons. Farming people from China gave their mummies tools and seeds for growing crops in the afterlife.

Many mummies have led their afterlives in private, lying peacefully in their tombs. Others have not been so lucky. The Incas, a people who lived in South America hundreds of years ago, brought out the mummies of their kings for display on special occasions.

The most famous mummies come from ancient Egypt. One reason Egyptian mummies are so famous is that there are so many of them. The ancient Egyptians left thousands and

The Incas of ancient South America sometimes killed and mummified people as sacrifices, or gifts, to the gods. In exchange for the sacrifices, the Incas hoped the gods would send them good weather or protect people from enemies. (Even if this worked, it was small comfort to the mummies themselves.)

thousands of mummies behind. And many Egyptian mummies were buried in pyramids, which are big and hard to ignore. And when it came to making up stories about mummies, either for books or movies, Egyptian mummies grabbed most of the early spotlight. And they've held onto it ever since.

The pyramids in Giza, Egypt, were built as final resting places for Egypt's kings. Many historians believe that the pyramid's shape held religious meaning for the ancient Egyptians.

2 Egypt Leads the Way

Egypt is a desert country, except for a narrow, fertile strip of land on both sides of the Nile River. The first

Egyptian villages date to about 3000 B.C.

The earliest Egyptians did not try to mummify their dead. They simply buried bodies in the desert sand, naked and with a few belongings. This process helped preserve the bodies naturally. The sand dried out the bodies and kept them from decaying. As early Egyptian mummies dried out, their skin started to look like a strong, tough paper called

Egypt is hot and dry—a natural place for preserving bodies. But how do you make a mummy in a cold place? It turns out that cold preserves a body just as well as heat does.

Some very cold places are covered in permafrost, a layer of frozen ground that never thaws, even in summer. Bodies buried a few feet down in the permafrost won't decay.

parchment. The skin stretched tightly over the mummies' skulls and gave their faces angry or scared expressions.

Eventually, the ancient Egyptians started to preserve bodies on purpose. They used a process called embalming. Embalmers drained the body of its natural fluids, such as blood. The embalmers then re-

The word *embalm* comes from a Latin word that means "sweet-smelling oil."

placed the body fluids with special chemical solutions. These solutions helped keep the body from decaying.

According to the ancient Egyptian religion, the god Anubis did the first embalming. The dearly departed was the god Osiris, who had been trampled to death by his jealous brother, Seth.

Of course, if embalming was good enough for the gods, it was good enough for the kings of Egypt too. Egypt's kings were called pharaohs. Embalming was so expensive at first that only the pharaohs could afford it.

But embalming wasn't the only expense in preparing bodies for the afterlife. Pharaohs also wanted big tombs to serve as their homes after death. About 2600 B.C., the pharaoh Djoser built the first Egyptian pyramid to serve as his tomb.

The ancient Egyptians believed in a life force called the *ka*. The ka was a spirit that

This mural of the god Anubis tending to a mummy appears on a tomb wall in Egypt. According to Egyptian religion, Anubis's most important role in the care of the dead was the weighing of the heart. If the heart was lighter than a feather, the body could pass on to the afterlife. If not, "the eater of souls" devoured the body.

lived inside everyone. Egyptians believed that the ka was separated from the body at death. But the ka still liked to stay close to the body. And in the tomb, the ka needed comforts that it had enjoyed in life. So Egyptians stocked their tombs with supplies such as tools, food, wine, clothing, furniture, gold, and jewels.

And pharaohs did not like the idea of spending eternity alone. They made sure they had company in the tomb. When they died, their servants were killed, mummified, and placed in the tomb with them—whether the servants wanted to go or not.

We know more about the Egyptians than about many other ancient peoples because they liked to write things down. Egyptian picture writing, called hieroglyphics *(above)*, gives us a lot of information about Egyptian customs and history.

After pharaohs began building pyramids, everyone was impressed—including grave robbers. The robbers broke into pyramids to steal the treasures they contained. Eventually, to prevent robbery, pharaohs started building their tombs in a secret cemetery. Built near the Nile River, the cemetery was called the Valley of the Kings. There was only one entrance to the cemetery, and soldiers guarded it.

THE SCIENCE OF MUMMIFICATION

The Egyptian mummy-making process went through changes over time. At first, the process left mummies covered in black shells. The black stuff looked like bitumen, a tarlike substance. The black stuff wasn't actually bitumen. But Egyptians began calling it by the Arabic word for bitumen, *mumiya*. In time, this became the English word *mummy*.

Over the centuries, mummification became more complicated. It took forty days to prepare the body properly. The Egyptians learned that if the liver, intestines, stomach, and lungs were left inside, a body would rot. So mummy makers removed these organs but placed them near the body in four jars. A different god watched over each organ to make sure nothing bad happened to it.

Canopic jars held the organs of a mummy's body. Many were carved into the likenesses of the Sons of Horus, the gods responsible for watching over each organ. The gods are *(from left to right):* Qebhsenuef (intestines), Duamutef (stomach), Hapy (lungs), and Imsety (liver).

DYING FOR A KING

The Greek historian Herodotus, born around 484 B.C., wrote about mummifying techniques used in the ancient kingdom of Scythia. To honor a dead king, the Scythians opened him up, cleaned out his body, and filled it with pleasant-smelling things such as parsley seeds and herbs. Then they sewed up the body and covered it in wax. The Scythians also buried each king with fifty horses and fifty loyal citizens. Both horses and people were killed and made into mummies.

This gold comb was found in a Scythian tomb.

Mummy makers also removed the brain. They did not remove the heart, however. The Egyptians believed the heart controlled thought and memory, which the dead person needed in the afterlife.

Once the organs were out, mummy makers covered the body with a natural salt. The salt helped the body dry out. After the body was dry, mummy makers wrapped it in linen bandages. They coated the bandages with perfumes and resins (sticky substances from plants). Bandaging a mummy took two weeks. This process was not something to be rushed. Finally, mummy makers placed the wrapped mummy in a painted coffin.

All this preparation was expensive. But as mummy makers became more experienced, the costs gradually came down. Besides the pharaohs, high priests and nobles (people of

Ancient Egyptians took great care to properly prepare their dead for the afterlife. In the image below, a priest wraps a dead body in strips of clean linen.

high or royal birth) started being mummified too. Later, the middle and lower classes joined in. Their tombs were more modest, though—usually just covered pits in the ground.

But the drop in cost didn't mean that mummification had become a one-size-fits-all process. Like modern-day funerals, mummification came in different price ranges. Some people could afford only to have their organs removed after death. But a body without its organs was hollow and sunken. It wasn't much to look at. It cost more to make the empty body look good again. For those who could

Many ancient Egyptian tombs have elaborate murals and carvings on the walls. These murals often tell stories about the person buried there, along with familiar tales from the *Book of the Dead*, a book about Egyptian beliefs in the afterlife. The tomb above is in Al Bawiti, Egypt.

afford it, mummy makers filled the empty body spaces with packing materials such as cloth and sawdust. Over the years, mummy makers also found better ways to preserve the skin.

Since death lasts so much longer than life, you might think the Egyptians would have been in a hurry to get it started. Actually, they weren't. They enjoyed life too much to want to cut it short. But the Egyptians were comforted knowing that when they died, they would be in good shape.

3 Mummies on the Move

Most Egyptians believed that mummification was a good thing. They went to a great deal of trouble and expense to have their bodies prepared for the afterlife.

They also carved signs on tomb walls, telling others to leave their graves alone. And just in case a warning was not enough, tomb builders created dead-end passageways and other booby traps to discourage intruders.

But that was as far as the Egyptians went. Modern-day stories and movies tell us that Egyptian mummies made curses and threatened to leave their tombs if they were ever disturbed. These ideas, however, didn't come from ancient Egypt. The ancient Egyptians had a complex religion filled with prayers, hymns, gods, and goddesses. The Egyptians wrote down many of their beliefs about the afterlife in a manuscript called the *Book of the Dead*. But the book says nothing about mummies making curses or having special powers.

Do Mummies Get the Proper Respect?

In the centuries after they were built, many Egyptian tombs were robbed of their valuables. But disrespecting mummies did not stop with grave robbing. Once the power of ancient

The idea of magic and curses in connection with mummies had its roots in the 600s, when Arab armies conquered Egypt. The Arabs believed in magic and curses. The Egyptians had thousands of ancient mummies. It took many centuries for the two ideas to come together in books and stories.

Egypt had weakened, people began to mistreat mummies themselves. Starting around the 1100s A.D., grave robbers started to steal mummies. They either boiled the mummies for the oils that would seep out of their bodies or ground them up to create potions. Both the oils and potions were highly valued as medicine. People believed they could cure everything from paralysis and poisoning to coughs and headaches.

Over the next few hundred years, the demand for mummy oils and potions grew. To meet the demand (and make the profits), some Egyptians began creating "instant mummies." These were fake mummies made from poor people who had recently died. To make the mummies look old, creators dunked the bandaged bodies in tar and dried them in the sun. The instant mummy-making practice lasted until around 1700, when buyers started to discover the fakes.

In 1798 a French general named Napoleon Bonaparte conquered

Egypt. Napoleon was interested in history and in Egyptian buildings such as the pyramids. Along with soldiers, he brought scientists, engineers, and artists with him to Egypt to study the ancient civilization. Afterward, writers made a series of books about the artwork and buildings that

Egyptology—the study of ancient Egypt—began after Napoleon (*below*) journeyed to Egypt in the late 1700s.

Napoleon's team had studied. Napoleon's interest put Egypt into the spotlight. Many Europeans also became interested in ancient Egyptian art, language, and architecture.

Still, almost nobody cared about mummies. To historians and other experts, a tomb containing jewelry or gold cups was valuable. But the mummies buried with this treasure were worthless.

People continued to treat mummies poorly. For instance, in the 1800s, an American papermaker from Maine bought brown linen

An explorer lifts a golden crown from Queen Khnemit's mummy in Dahshur, Egypt, in the 1890s.

mummy wrappings to use in his business. But he found that the linen was too dark to be made into fine white writing paper. So the paper-maker made the linen into brown wrapping paper instead.

In *The Innocents Abroad* (1869), American writer Mark Twain tells how Egyptian railroad engineers used old mummies for fuel. The engineers stacked the mummies like wood and tossed them into the train's boiler as needed. Twain notes that one engineer told his coworker to stop passing him the mummies of common people. "They don't burn worth a cent," the man said. "Pass out a king!"

Fortunately for the remaining mummies, the situation was changing. Some people were gaining a new respect for the ancient world. However, not everyone held this view. A lot of people weren't archaeologists (scientists who study the remains of past human cultures) and didn't care to be. So tomb robberies continued. But at least some people were trying to preserve the past.

The American horror writer Edgar Allan Poe published the short story "Some Words with a Mummy" in 1850. In this clever tale, a mummy brought back to life discusses life in ancient Egypt and learns about life in the 1800s.

MUMMIES BREAK OUT

Ancient Egypt's rich history was also stirring some imaginations. Writers began to include mummies in their books and stories. One of the first mummy stories was Jane Webb Loudon's *The Mummy! A Tale of the Twenty-Second Century*. Published in 1827, the book was set in Great Britain three hundred years in the future. The story mixed advanced technology with the tale of a mummy that comes back to life.

In 1880 Grant Allen (writing as J. Arbuthnot Wilson) published a story called "My New Year's Eve among the Mummies." In it, a British man finds a hidden entrance to a pyramid. He explores further and comes upon a pharaoh and his attendants. It seems they come alive for one day every thousand years. And that day is today. This fact is remarkable. But it's not necessarily dangerous—until the main character becomes attracted to the pharaoh's daughter. Then, not surprisingly, problems arise.

Magic played a part in Sir Arthur Conan Doyle's story "Lot No. 249," published in 1892. Doyle was most famous for creating and writing about the detective Sherlock Holmes. But this story concerned a mummy sold at auction (labeled Lot No. 249 by the auctioneers). The up-to-no-good buyer is Edward Bellingham. Soon Bellingham is using dark magic to bring the mummy back to life to murder people.

In his later years, Sir Arthur Conan Doyle became very interested in the spirit world. He was particularly interested in communicating with the dead.

"Lot No. 249" was one of the first stories to make mummies evil—even if it really wasn't their fault.

Bram Stoker, the author of the vampire novel *Dracula*, introduced another popular mummy theme. In *The Jewel of Seven Stars* (1904), he wrote of an ancient Egyptian queen whose soul inhabits the body of a living person. Stoker mentioned no mummies, but his themes of ancient Egyptian royalty and one person's soul living inside another person's body would not be forgotten. Like mummies themselves, these ideas were bound to have a long afterlife.

4 ARE YOU MY MUMMY?

Despite a good story here and there, mummies were not very popular in the early 1900s. Writers and readers were much more interested in stories about vampires and ghosts than in tales about mummies. While mummies were interesting, people couldn't make a personal connection with them. Mummies seemed far away and unfamiliar, especially to people in Europe and the United States.

INTRODUCING KING TUT

That all changed in the 1920s, when Egypt's young King Tutankhamen, more commonly known as King Tut, reappeared on the scene. We say reappeared because, of course, King Tut had lived in Egypt before— more than three thousand years earlier. The king had died in 1352 B.C.

Late in 1922, the English archaeologist Howard Carter discovered the location of Tutankhamen's tomb in the Valley of the Kings. Carter did not stumble on the tomb by accident. He had been searching for it for eight years. Many people believed that all the tombs in the Valley of the Kings had been found by then. But Carter was not convinced, and his hunch proved to be correct. A few weeks later, in February 1923, Carter and his workers opened the tomb.

The tomb that Carter found had been almost completely untouched since ancient times. If

Archaeologists open Tutankhamen's tomb in Egypt in 1923.

The mummy of King Tut was placed in a series of nesting coffins and boxes. The coffins are gold or wood covered in gold foil. Each is carved to look like the figure of Tut. The outer coffin figure (*right*) wears a cobra headpiece.

grave robbers had ever disturbed it, they had not done much damage. In Europe and the United States, the tomb caused a sensation. Certainly, the jewels and other treasures buried with the king were very valuable. But the opportunity to study a tomb in almost perfect condition was also priceless.

Since King Tut was a mummy, curiosity about mummies rose to a new high. For Americans and Europeans, ancient Egypt had always seemed like a distant and mysterious place. Yet here was a small piece of Egypt that everyone could learn about through photographs and news stories. Added to that was a juicy detail: it looked like Tut had been killed by a blow to the head (modern-day X-rays showed this theory to be false, however).

Maybe the rumor of Tut's murder gave mummies a bad name. But from that moment on, they never were the good guys. You'd think all that sleep would make mummies well rested and cheerful. It didn't. According to storytellers, mummies came back from the dead for two reasons. One was for revenge, usually on the people who had robbed their tombs. The other was to be reunited with someone, usually a long-lost love.

MUMMIES TAKE TO THE SILVER SCREEN

Early moviemakers had already introduced Dracula and Frankenstein to the big screen. Mummies seemed like another good bet. The most popular of the early movies was *The Mummy* (1932). It starred Boris Karloff, who had achieved fame playing the monster in *Frankenstein* (1931). In *The Mummy*, Karloff played an ancient Egyptian priest named Imhotep, who had been buried alive. How had he earned this gruesome death? Well, the princess he loved had died, and he had committed the crime of trying to bring her back to life.

One of the first short movies featuring a mummy plot was *Cléopâtre* (1899), created by French filmmaker Georges Méliès. The movie concerned an old man who chops up a mummy hoping to use the pieces to bring a woman back to life.

The film begins in ancient Egypt. Then the action shifts to modern times, where archaeologists read aloud a magical spell. Although they are unaware of it, this spell brings Imhotep back to life. He becomes

A LOVE THAT DEFIED TIME
DRIVES A BEAUTIFUL
GIRL TO HER DOOM!

KARLOFF THE UNCANNY

IN

"The MUMMY"

WITH
ZITA JOHANN · DAVID MANNERS
EDWARD VAN SLOAN · ARTHUR BYRON.

a successful businessman in Cairo, Egypt. Then he discovers that the soul of his beloved princess is inside the body of a living woman. This news should make him happy, but Egyptian priests are hard to please. Imhotep is not content to leave the princess's soul where it is. He wants it back in its original body. (And he also wants that body back in its original condition.) He sets about to make these things happen.

More than seventy mummy movies have been made worldwide. The movie poster above is from the popular 1932 film *The Mummy*.

Audiences loved *The Mummy*, and its success led to a number of sequels from Universal Studios. These movies included *The Mummy's Hand* (1940), *The Mummy's Tomb* (1942), *The Mummy's Ghost* (1944), and *The Mummy's Curse* (1944). The mummy was never happy in these films, and he made a lot of other people pretty miserable too.

This publicity photo from *The Mummy's Ghost* (1944) shows the mummy (played by Lon Chaney Jr.) carrying off a woman he believes to have the soul of his Egyptian princess.

In the 1950s, Hammer Film Productions in Great Britain began to update films about Dracula and Frankenstein. But it made sure not to neglect the mummy. Its version of *The Mummy* (1959) starred Christopher Lee. He didn't have any lines, but his half-decayed face was a picture easily worth a thousand words. This film was followed by *The Curse of the Mummy's Tomb* (1964), *The Mummy's Shroud* (1967), and *Blood from the Mummy's Tomb* (1971). Some people think we should leave mummies to rest in peace, but apparently these people just don't go to the movies.

Paul Preston (played by David Bock) strikes at the mummy (played by Eddie Powell) in the 1967 film *The Mummy's Shroud.*

MUMMIES AND MORE MUMMIES

In modern times, writers have produced mummy short stories, mummy comic books, and mummy novels. Horror writer Anne Rice is best known

Bram Stoker never wrote about mummies. But this didn't keep filmmakers from coming out with *Bram Stoker's The Mummy* (1997). Since Stoker died in 1912, the filmmakers probably thought they were safe from revenge. Given the subject matter, though, this may not have been a wise move. You never know when the dead might take offense.

for books about vampires, but she also wrote *The Mummy or Ramses the Damned* (1989). The emphasis here is more on romance than horror. Rice's Ramses would probably feel at home on one of TV's afternoon soap operas.

Mummies have appeared in children's books too. R. L. Stine used the mummy theme twice in his Goosebumps series and in some other books as well. In *The Mummy, the Will, and the Crypt* (1983) by John Bellairs, twelve-year-old Johnny

Dixon and his friend Professor Childermass deal with all three things mentioned in the title. If there's such a thing as good-natured horror, Bellairs can write it. His mummy is not a bad guy. He just looks bad because he's under the power of an evil person.

Modern-day movies have given the mummy new life. *Tales from the*

Of television's cartoon heroes, Scooby-Doo and Jonny Quest have both faced mummified enemies. In both cases, the mummy is not a freethinking individual. He is under the power or spell of someone else.

Darkside: The Movie (1990) was a British film. One segment of the movie is a takeoff on Arthur Conan Doyle's "Lot No. 249." In the segment, a mummy causes trouble—and death—at a university.

The Mummy of 1999 was the first feature film on the subject of mummies to make full use of computer-generated graphics. These graphics are noticeable in many scenes, including ones showing thousands of scarab beetles skittering through a tomb.

In *The Mummy* (1999), Brendan Fraser is the bold adventurer Rick O'Connell. Rachel Weisz is Evelyn Carnahan, a shy librarian who soon shows her true toughness. As in other mummy movies, ancient lovers have been separated, dead people come back to life, and innocent

A scary scene from the 1999 version of *The Mummy*, featuring High Priest Imhotep (played by Arnold Vosloo)

bystanders better watch out. The movie's computer-generated special effects created scary scenes that kept many viewers from sleeping well afterward.

In *The Mummy Returns* (2001), Fraser and Weisz return along with their bandage-bound enemy. Ten years have passed. Rick and Evelyn have married each other. They are living in London, England, with their eight-year-old son, Alex. The Mummy is also in London, being studied in the British Museum. Certain events wake the Mummy again. Rick and Evelyn must stop him before he can raise the army of an ancient warrior, the Scorpion King.

The latest version of *The Mummy* and *The Mummy Returns (above)* earned more than $800 million at the box office worldwide.

The success of mummy movies shows that even after thousands of years, mummies are still a force in our lives. The question is, How many mummies remain to go on the rampage? The answer is unknown, but it may well lie in some dusty or buried portion of the *Book of the Dead*. Then again, the predictions there can be pretty unreliable. One thing seems certain, though. As long as there are people—grave robbers, archaeologists, explorers—who disturb the remains of the dead, this act will surely haunt them, and us, for many years to come.

SOURCE NOTE

29 Mark Twain, "The Innocents Abroad, Vol. II," *The Unabridged Mark Twain* (Philadelphia: Running Press, 1976), 377.

SELECTED BIBLIOGRAPHY

Andrews, Carol. *Egyptian Mummies*. Cambridge, MA: Harvard University Press, 1984.

Aufderheide, Arthur C. *The Scientific Study of Mummies*. Cambridge, UK: Cambridge University Press, 2003.

Cowie, Susan D., and Tom Johnson. *The Mummy in Fact, Fiction and Film*. Jefferson, NC: MacFarland & Company, Inc., 2002.

Halliwell, Leslie. *The Dead That Walk: Dracula, Frankenstein, the Mummy and Other Favorite Movie Monsters*. New York: Continuum Publishing, 1986.

Leca, Ange-Perre. *The Egyptian Way of Death: Mummies and the Cult of the Immortal*. Garden City, NY: Doubleday and Company, 1981.

El Mahdy, Christine. *Mummies, Myth and Magic in Ancient Egypt*. New York: Thames and Hudson, 1989.

Reid, Howard. *In Search of the Immortals: Mummies, Death and the Afterlife*. New York: St. Martin's Press, 2001.

FURTHER READING AND WEBSITES

Bellairs, John. *The Mummy, the Will, and the Crypt*. New York: Puffin Books, 2004. First published in 1983 by Dial Books. In this mystery novel, twelve-year-old Johnny Dixon is determined to find a lost will and collect the reward. But searching for the will involves going into the creepy, deserted Glomus mansion. Johnny soon finds that he is not alone in the mansion—he must fight off a monstrous mummy.

Campbell, Caroline. "The World's Best Mummies." *Travel Channel.com.*
http://travel.discovery.com/fansites/worldsbest/mummies/mummies.html
The Travel Channel's fansite lists nine of the most interesting and un-
usual mummies—created by humans and nature—from all over the world,
from Moscow's Red Square to an Irish church to the mountains of Peru.

Day, Nancy. *Your Travel Guide to Ancient Egypt.* Minneapolis: Twenty-
First Century Books, 2001. Learn all about ancient Egypt in this fun
"travel guide."

Deem, James M. *Bodies from the Bog.* Boston: Houghton Mifflin, 2003.
The bogs of northern Europe have kept human bodies preserved for many
centuries. Discovering the mummies—and what they were buried with—
gives archaeologists a glimpse into life two and three thousand years ago.
With engaging text and many photographs, Deem discusses the mysteries of the bog people. How did they die? Why did they die? And how have
they been so well preserved?

"Entering King Tut's Tomb, 1923," *EyeWitness to History.*
http://www.eyewitnesstohistory.com/tut.htm
This website offers a detailed account of Howard Carter's discovery of
King Tut's tomb, with extensive quotes from Carter's own writings. Also
included is a diagram of the tomb and information on the origin of the
legend of "King Tut's Curse."

"How to Make a Mummy," *National Geographic.com.*
http://www.nationalgeographic.com/tv/mummy/
This website takes you step-by-step through the ancient Egyptian
mummy-making process. Photos and illustrations explain what Egyptian
embalmers did with the mummy's internal organs, how salt was used in the
process, and how the mummy was wrapped.

"Unraveling the Mysteries of King Tutankhamun." *National Geographic.com.* http://magma.nationalgeographic.com/ngm/tut/mysteries/index.html The pharaoh awaits curious visitors on this interactive website. The interior of the tomb, the royal coffins and mummy, and the high-tech science used to study Tut are all detailed. The science section also includes a reconstruction of Tut's skull, showing viewers what the king may have looked like in real life.

Wilcox, Charlotte. *Mummies, Bones, & Body Parts.* Minneapolis: Carolrhoda Books, Inc., 2000. Wilcox looks at burial and mummification practices from around the world. She explores how archaeologists study mummified remains and examines the objects buried with mummies. Vivid, and sometimes grim, photos highlight this book.

Yerkow, Lila Perl. *Mummies, Tombs and Treasure: Secrets of Ancient Egypt.* Illustrated by Erika Weihs. New York: Clarion Books, 1990. This book provides a thorough introduction to Egyptian religion, history, and mummification practices. Diagrams, photographs, and maps accompany the text.

MOVIES

The Mummy—The Legacy Collection. Universal City, CA: Universal Studios, 2004. This boxed DVD set offers five classic mummy films from the 1930s and 1940s: *The Mummy, The Mummy's Hand, The Mummy's Tomb, The Mummy's Ghost,* and *The Mummy's Curse.* Acting great Boris Karloff stars in the original *Mummy,* while Lon Chaney takes the spotlight in three of the four sequels.

The Mummy Collection. Universal City, CA: Universal Studies, 2002. This DVD collection includes Brendan Fraser and Rachel Weisz in *The Mummy* and *The Mummy Returns.* The collection is loaded with extras, such as facts about ancient Egypt and a look at the films' masterful special effects.

INDEX

Anubis, 16, 17

bogs, 10
Bonaparte, Napoleon, 26–28
Book of the Dead, 26, 43

Carter, Howard, 34
cost of mummification, 21–23

Egypt, 8, 12–13, 25, 33, 34–35; climate of, 14, 15; history of, 13, 15, 26, 27, 28; in literature, 29, 31; in movies, 36, 37
Egyptian mummification, 15–19, 21–23, 24–26; and beliefs about the afterlife, 17–18, 24, 25–26
embalming, 16–17

Great Britain, 8, 29, 39

Incas, 12
Innocents Abroad, The (1869), 28
"instant mummies," 26
Italian Alps, 8

Jewel of Seven Stars, The (1904), 31

ka, 17–18

"Lot No. 249" (1892), 30–31, 41

mummies: defined, 8; history of, 8, 10–13; locations of, 8, 9, 10; mistreatment of, 26, 28–29; modern-day, 11; in movies, 36–39, 40–42; preservation of, 15; in stories and books, 29–31, 32, 40; on TV, 40; types of, 10; word origin, 19

Mummy! A Tale of the Twenty-Second Century, The (1827), 29
Mummy, The (1932), 36–38
Mummy, The (1959), 39
Mummy, The (1999), 41
Mummy, the Will, and the Crypt, The (1983), 40
Mummy or Ramses the Damned, The (1989), 40
Mummy Returns, The (2001), 42
Mummy's Ghost, The (1944), 38
Mummy's Shroud, The (1967), 39
"My New Year's Eve among the Mummies" (1880), 30

Napoleon. *See* Bonaparte, Napoleon

pyramids, 13

Scythian mummification, 20
"Some Words with a Mummy" (1850), 29

Tales from the Darkside: The Movie (1990), 40–41
Tutankhamen, (king), 33, 34–36

Valley of the Kings, 18, 34

ABOUT THE AUTHOR

Stephen Krensky is the author of many fiction and nonfiction books for children, including titles in the On My Own Folklore series and *Frankenstein*, *Werewolves*, *Dragons*, *Vampires*, and *Bigfoot*. When he isn't hunched over his computer, he makes school visits and teaches writing workshops. In his free time, he enjoys playing tennis and softball and reading books by other people. Krensky lives in Massachusetts with his wife, Joan, and their family.

PHOTO ACKNOWLEDGMENTS

The images in this book are used with the permission of: © Stephen L. Alvarez/National Geographic/Getty Images, p. 1; © Universal International Pictures/Photofest, pp. 2-3; © EPA/SIPA, p. 9; © Chris Lisle/CORBIS, p. 10; © Hulton Archive/Getty Images, p. 11; © Reuters/CORBIS, p. 12; © age fotostock/SuperStock, pp. 13, 19; © Yann Arthus-Bertrand/CORBIS, p. 16; © SuperStock, Inc./SuperStock, p. 17; © Ben Mangor/SuperStock, p. 18; © Charles O'Rear/CORBIS, p. 20; © Bettmann/CORBIS, p. 21; © Ron Watts/CORBIS, p. 22; © Swim Ink 2, LLC/CORBIS, p. 27; © North Wind Picture Archives, p. 28; © Keystone/Getty Images, p. 30; © Hulton-Deutsch Collection/CORBIS, p. 34; © Ethan Miller/Getty Images, p. 35; © Photofest, p. 37; Courtesy of Universal Studios Licensing, LLLP. Image provided by Bettmann/CORBIS, p. 38; "The Mummy's Shroud" © 1967 Twentieth Century Fox. All rights reserved. Image provided by Photofest, p. 39; Courtesy of Universal Studios Licensing, LLLP. Image provided by Photofest, pp. 41, 42; Illustrations by Bill Hauser, pp. 6-7, 14-15, 24-25, 32-33, 43; All page backgrounds illustrated by Bill Hauser.

Cover illustration by Bill Hauser.